# THE COMPLETE GUIDE TO FRENCH BULLDOGS

David Anderson

Copyright © 2018 David Anderson
All rights reserved.

# TABLE OF CONTENTS

**CHAPTER 1**
Introduction . . . . . . . . . . . . . . . . . . . . . . . . 6

**CHAPTER 2**
Understanding French Bulldogs . . . . . . . . . 8
a.) What is a French Bulldog? . . . . . . . . . . . . . 9
b.) French Bulldog History . . . . . . . . . . . . . . . 12
c.) French Bulldog vs. Regular Bulldogs . . . . . 14

**CHAPTER 3**
Picking a French Bulldog Puppy . . . . . . . . 16
a.) Where to Look for French Bulldog Puppies . . . 16
b.) Choosing a Responsible Breeder . . . . . . . . 18
c.) Picking a Healthy French Bulldog Puppy . . . 20

**CHAPTER 4**
Adopting a French Bulldog . . . . . . . . . . . . 22
a.) Pros and Cons of Adopting a Dog . . . . . . . 22
b.) French Bulldog Puppies vs. Adults . . . . . . 24
c.) Tips for Adopting a Dog . . . . . . . . . . . . . . 25

**CHAPTER 5**
Preparing Your Home . . . . . . . . . . . . . . . . 26
a.) Puppy-Proofing Indoors and Out . . . . . . . 27
b.) Dangerous Foods for Your Frenchie . . . . . 28
c.) French Bulldogs and Other Pets . . . . . . . . 29
d.) Preparing a Space for Your Frenchie . . . . . 30

**CHAPTER 6**
The First Few Days at Home . . . . . . . . . . . 32
a.) Getting Kids Ready for a Puppy . . . . . . . . 32
b.) Initial Supplies and Accessories . . . . . . . . 34
c.) Riding Home from the Breeder . . . . . . . . . 35
d.) The First Night at Home . . . . . . . . . . . . . 36
e.) Your Frenchie's First Vet Visit . . . . . . . . . . 37

**CHAPTER 7**
## The First Month at Home ........................... 38
a.) Enforcing House Rules ................................. 39
b.) Early Socialization Tips ................................ 39
c.) Picking a Training Method ............................ 40
d.) Cost Breakdown of the First Year ................... 40

**CHAPTER 8**
## Housetraining Your French Bulldog Puppy ........ 44
a.) Inside or Outside? ...................................... 44
b.) Keeping an Eye on Your Puppy ....................... 46
c.) Treats for Good Behavior ............................. 46
d.) Crate Training Tips and Tricks ....................... 48

**CHAPTER 9**
## Socializing Your Frenchie ......................... 50
a.) Things to Incorporate in Socialization ............. 51
b.) Noise Conditioning .................................... 52
c.) Teaching Bite Inhibition ............................. 54
d.) Proper Behavior at the Dog Park .................... 54

**CHAPTER 10**
## Being the Best Puppy Parent ...................... 56
a.) Don't Reward Bad Behavior .......................... 57
b.) Tips for Dealing with Problem Behavior ............ 58
c.) Preventing Separation Anxiety ...................... 59

**CHAPTER 11**
## Training Your French Bulldog ..................... 60
a.) When Should You Start Training? .................... 61
b.) Dos and Don'ts for Dog Training .................... 61
c.) Using Food Rewards ................................... 62
d.) Puppy Preschool – Yay or Nay? ...................... 62

**CHAPTER 12**
## Teaching the Basics ............................... 64
a.) Why is Obedience Important? ........................ 65
b.) Sit, Down, Come and Stay ............................ 65
c.) Taking Your Training Up A Notch .................... 67

**CHAPTER 13**
## Feeding Your French Bulldog ............................................. 68
a.) Why is a Healthy Diet Important? ........................... 68
b.) Canine Nutritional Needs ......................................... 70
c.) Choosing a Healthy Dog Food ................................. 71
d.) The Dangers of Obesity ............................................ 73

**CHAPTER 14**
## Grooming Your French Bulldog ........................................ 74
a.) Recommended Grooming Tools ............................... 74
b.) Brushing and Bathing ................................................ 75
c.) Trimming the Nails .................................................... 76
d.) Cleaning Your Dog's Ears ......................................... 76
e.) Brushing Your Frenchie's Teeth ............................... 76

**CHAPTER 15**
## French Bulldog Healthcare ............................................... 78
a.) Routine Veterinary Care ............................................ 79
b.) Preventing Fleas and Ticks ....................................... 80
c.) What is Heartworm? .................................................. 81
d.) Vaccinating Your Frenchie ........................................ 81
e.) Common Frenchie Health Problems ....................... 82

**CHAPTER 16**
## Travel Tips for Frenchies ................................................... 84
a.) Basic Car Safety Tips ................................................. 85
b.) Traveling with Your Frenchie ................................... 86
c.) Home Away from Home ............................................ 86
d.) Kennels vs. Pet Sitters ................................................ 87
## Conclusion ............................................................................ 88

## CHAPTER 1

# Introduction

Photo Courtesy of Jennifer Aitchison

All dogs are not created equal. With hundreds of different breeds on the planet, how could they be? Every dog owner has his or her own preferences, but one breed that stands head and shoulders above many breeds is the French Bulldog. With a maximum height of 12 inches, these little dogs don't literally stand above most of the dog breeds out there, but they are definitely a unique and wonderful breed that is worth considering.

The French Bulldog is by far one of the spunkiest, most lovable dog breeds on the planet. These dogs may be small but they are full of personality and they have endless love and loyalty to give. Like any dog, however, French Bulldogs do require a significant investment of time and money. Unless you are able to commit to giving your Frenchie the best life it could have for the entirety of its lifespan, you should consider another pet.

They say that dog is a man's best friend and no breed exemplifies this saying more than the French Bulldog. If you are thinking about getting one of these wonderful little dogs for yourself, congratulations! But before you make up your mind, take the time to learn everything you can about these little dogs to ensure that you have the time, the passion, and the money to devote to its care and keeping. In this book, you will find all of the information you need to know to ensure that you become the best French Bulldog owner you can be.

# CHAPTER 1 Introduction

*Photo Courtesy of Sean Bunevich*

## CHAPTER 2

# Understanding French Bulldogs

Also known lovingly as the "Frenchie," the French Bulldog is ranked among the top 15 breeds in the United States according to AKC registration statistics. These dogs may be small, but they are full of spunk and personality – that is what makes them so popular. Frenchies are some of the best companion dogs out there and they are also a great choice for apartments, condos, and other small living spaces.

If you are looking for a smaller breed that isn't short on love and loyalty, the French Bulldog might be the right choice for you. In this chapter, you'll learn all about the breed and its history, so you can decide whether this breed might be your perfect match.

*Photo Courtesy of Laura Taylor*

CHAPTER 2   Understanding French Bulldogs

# a.) What is a French Bulldog?

> *French Bulldogs are clowns and their personality is so entertaining that is brings a whole new light into your home!"*
>
> *Linda*
> *lovabullfrenchies.com*

The French Bulldog is a small companion breed known for its short stature, stocky build, and bat-like ears. These little dogs may look strange to some, but they have a unique beauty about them – both inside and out. Frenchies are intelligent and loyal dogs, forming close bonds with all members of the family, including kids, household pets, and other dogs. Quite simply, they are one of the top choices for dog lovers looking for a small dog.

The average height for a full-grown French Bulldog is between 11 and 12 inches at the shoulder, and they generally weigh between 16 and 28 pounds at maturity. These dogs are small in comparison to many breeds, but they have a substantial build and well-defined muscles. According to the AKC standard for the breed, French Bulldogs have the appearance of "an active, intelligent, muscular dog of heavy bone, smooth coat, compactly built, and of medium or small structure". But the Frenchie is so much more than that.

These little dogs may not be glamorous, but what they lack in aesthetic appeal they make up for in personality. The French Bulldog is full of energy and loves to play, though it is not inherently hyperactive. This breed thrives on human contact and will be just as happy napping on the couch with you as chasing a ball in the yard. In fact, Frenchies are not known for having high energy levels or demanding needs for exercise – another trait that makes them a great indoor dog.

In addition to their low exercise requirements, French Bulldogs are a low-maintenance breed in other ways. For example, their short coat is easy to groom and doesn't require any trimming. Their ears stand erect so there is a low risk for ear infections, and they don't tend to bark as much as other breeds. There are some important maintenance tasks you will need to perform, however, that are very different from other breeds.

The French Bulldog is what is known as a brachycephalic breed – this term simply refers to the dog's shortened facial structure. In addition to having a shortened snout, the Frenchie also has wrinkles on its face and sometimes in the skin covering its body. These folds of skin can accumulate moisture which may harbor infection-causing bacteria, so you'll need to check your Frenchie's folds frequently to make sure they are clean and dry. You'll also have to be careful to make sure your Frenchie doesn't overheat and that it isn't subjected to rigorous exercise – its shortened face can cause breathing difficulties which may be exacerbated in these situations.

As far as personality goes, the French Bulldog is the ultimate goofball. These dogs absolutely adore spending time with their families and they can turn anything into a game. This is not a breed that does well when left alone for long periods of time – French Bulldogs are highly prone to separation anxiety and may develop destructive behaviors if they don't get enough attention. For this reason, some French Bulldog owners get a second dog so they can keep each other company (but this shouldn't be a replacement for spending quality time with your pup).

Because the French Bulldog is an intelligent breed, training is usually fairly easy. The key is to make sure that you clearly communicate what you expect from your dog so that your dog can deliver. When it does, be generous with your praise (and don't forget the treats) to reinforce the behavior. Your Frenchie wants to please you, so let it! Try to keep your training sessions short, about ten to fifteen minutes, so it doesn't get bored and stop paying attention.

In terms of health, the French Bulldog has an average lifespan of 11 to 14 years which is on par for dogs of its size. However, the Frenchie is prone to a number of serious health problems, many of which are hereditary – this means that responsible breeding practices are incredibly important. Some of the conditions to which this breed is prone include hip dysplasia, allergies, patellar luxation, intervertebral disc disease, von Willebrand's disease, elongated soft palate, and brachycephalic syndrome.

When it comes to color and patterns, many French Bulldogs exhibit a brindle pattern, though various shades of cream, fawn, and gray are also common. French Bulldogs sometimes have a black mask on the face and may also have other spots or white markings. The eyes for this breed are always dark, and the nose is usually black except in some light-colored dogs. Frenchies have a short coat that is fine in texture and smooth, with a short tail either straight or screwed. The ears are wide at the base and rounded at the tip, a shape usually referred to as "bat ear".

CHAPTER 2 Understanding French Bulldogs

# French Bulldog Breed Overview

**AKC Group:** non-sporting group

**Breed Size:** small

**Height:** 11 to 12 inches

**Weight:** 16 to 28 pounds

**Coat Length:** short

**Coat Texture:** moderately fine, smooth; skin is soft and loose, wrinkles on the face, head, and shoulders

**Color:** brindle, fawn, white, brindle and white; any color except solid black, mouse, liver, black and tan, black and white, and white with black

**Eyes and Nose:** eyes are dark in color, wideset, moderate in size; nose is black except in light-colored dogs

**Ears:** broad at the base, round top (bat ear); carried erect

Photo Courtesy of Crystal Myrholm

**Tail:** either straight or screwed; short

**Temperament:** loving, playful, smart, goofy, fun-loving

**Strangers:** quick to make friends, not inherently suspicious of strangers

**Other Dogs:** generally gets along well

**Other Pets:** generally not a problem (low prey drive)

**Training:** very smart, strong desire to please, positive reinforcement training is highly effective

**Exercise Needs:** moderately low, daily walk is adequate

**Health Conditions:** hip dysplasia, allergies, patellar luxation, intervertebral disc disease, von Willebrand's disease, elongated soft palate, and brachycephalic syndrome

**Lifespan:** average 11 to 14 years

## b.) French Bulldog History

The history of the French Bulldog breed is a little convoluted because there are several different stages of breed development spanning across three countries – England, France, and the United States. The foundation for the modern breed, the Bulldog, comes from England; but the smaller bulldog that came to be known as the French type was, of course, developed in France. But American breeders set the standard that came to include the now typical "bat ear".

The origins of the French Bulldog can be traced back some 150 to 200 years. The Bulldog was a strong, athletic breed with a muscular build that became popular for use in bull-baiting, a practice that is now outlawed. At the time, however, Bulldog breeders began to change the breed by crossing it with other breeds to make the Bulldog a bigger, heavier dog with more exaggerated features. Some breeders also crossed the Bulldog with terrier breeds to improve its skills in ratting and dogfighting.

Another group of breeders started to breed the Bulldog down in size, aiming for a lighter "toy" version of the breed weighing no more than 25 pounds. They also bred selectively in favor of physical traits including the erect ear, round forehead, and undershot jaw. There may have also been some crossing with terrier breeds to increase the liveliness of the smaller Bulldog. This version of the breed was particularly popular among workers, especially artisans in the lace-making industry.

As the smaller version of the Bulldog became more popular in society, the French began to take notice. Late in the 19th century, French breeders began to develop a more uniform version of the smaller Bulldog – it had a compact body with short, straight legs without the extreme undershot jaw exhibited by the larger Bulldog. Some of these smaller dogs had erect bat-like ears while others had rose ears. When wealthy American travelers visiting France fell in love with the breed, they began taking the dogs back to the USA where selective breeding continued.

The first French Bulldog was exhibited at the Westminster dog show in 1896 and it was featured on the cover of the Westminster catalog the following year. At the time, however, the AKC had not yet approved the breed so there was no formal standard. Some Frenchies continued to exhibit rose ears, though the bat ear was becoming more and more popular. This bothered American fanciers of the breed so they began the French Bulldog Club of America and quickly established a standard that

CHAPTER 2  Understanding French Bulldogs

*Photo Courtesy of Nicole Roy*

only allowed for the bat ear. In 1898, however, both bat-eared and rose-eared versions of the breed were still eligible for show at the Westminster dog show.

American fanciers were so outraged, in fact, that they withdrew their dogs and organized their own show – a show that only allowed for bat-eared dogs. The champion of this first show was a brindle French Bulldog named Dimboolaa. After the show, popularity of the breed skyrocketed in the United States, especially among East Coast society women. Following the First World War, however, the breed began to decline – the rise in popularity of the Boston Terrier may have played a role. Numbers for the breed may have also been low because natural French Bulldog births are notoriously difficult and it would be years before veterinary caesarean sections could be performed safely and routinely.

The popularity of the French Bulldog continued to decline throughout the Great Depression during the 1930s, though a small number of breeders in the United States and Europe fought to keep the breed alive. The breed continued to struggle during the Second World War but interest was renewed in the 1950s when Amanda West, a breeder from Detroit, began showing cream Frenchies; she was a huge success. Over time, cream and fawn colored Frenchies became more and more common at Westminster and other dog shows, though numbers were still low into the 1960s.

In the 1980s, the French Bulldog Club of America renewed its efforts to promote the breed. Younger breeders entered the scene and turned specialty shows into large-scale events – they also created a magazine devoted solely to the French Bulldog breed. Registrations continued to rise, topping 5,000 in 2006. Today, French Bulldogs are among the top fifteen most popular breeds in America according to AKC registration statistics and they continue to gain popularity with each passing year.

## c.) French Bulldog vs. Regular Bulldogs

You've already learned about the illustrious history of the French Bulldog, but you may still be wondering about how this breed differs from its predecessor, the Bulldog. The name Bulldog is actually given to two separate breeds – the American Bulldog and the English Bulldog. Both of these modern breeds were developed from the Old English Bulldog, the same dog that contributed to the development of the modern French Bulldog.

CHAPTER 2   Understanding French Bulldogs

The Bulldog is a medium-sized dog having a stocky build, wrinkled skin, and a shortened face. An English Bulldog typically weighs 40 to 60 pounds and there is no height standard for the breed. American Bulldogs stand up to 26 inches tall and can weigh as much as 120 pounds at maturity. Though they may have an intimidating look, both Bulldog breeds make excellent family pets. They are gentle in nature and love to spend time with their loved ones. They do, however, tend to be a little aloof around strangers and can be very protective.

Compared to the English and American Bulldog, the French Bulldog is smaller in size and has erect ears, rather than flop ears. None of the Bulldog breeds is particularly energetic, though they are all playful and loyal pets. In addition to being larger than the other Bulldog breeds, the American Bulldog is also more active and energetic. These dogs can jump surprisingly high and they are able to get into a lot of mischief if not properly supervised. They are never inherently aggressive, however, and they can get along well with family pets when they are raised together from a young age.

Photo Courtesy of Michael Barnes

## CHAPTER 3

# Picking a French Bulldog Puppy

Now that you know a little bit more about what makes the French Bulldog such a unique breed, you are well on your way to deciding whether or not this is the right breed for you. Having an understanding about the breed's history and some basic facts about temperament and personality are very important when choosing a dog. You also have to think about the practical aspects, however, and that's what you are going to learn in this chapter. Here you will find valuable information about where to find French Bulldog puppies, how to select a responsible breeder, and how to pick a healthy Frenchie puppy from a litter.

## a.) Where to Look for French Bulldog Puppies

If you are an animal lover, you are probably familiar with the pet stores in your area – you may even be a frequent visitor. If so, you've probably been inside at least one pet store that sells puppies. This being the case, you might assume that when you are ready to start shopping around for French Bulldog puppies that the pet store would be the best place to start. There are several reasons, however, to exercise some caution.

One of the biggest reasons to avoid buying a puppy at the pet store is that you don't know exactly where it came from. When you hold that wiggly little French Bulldog puppy in your arms it is easy to fall in love and to throw caution to the wind. But, in this case, what you don't know could hurt you. Many pet stores do not provide buyers with records of where the puppies come from. This means that you don't know anything about the puppy's parentage and breeding, which means that you are in the dark when it comes to inherited health problems. This is particularly dangerous with the French Bulldog because this breed is prone to a number of serious congenital diseases.

While it is entirely possible that your local pet store gets puppies from responsible breeders, it is fairly unlikely. Many pet stores get their puppies from puppy mills, and there is no way to tell where a puppy

CHAPTER 3 Picking a French Bulldog Puppy

came from just by looking at it. The Humane Society estimates that there are as many as 10,000 puppy mills in the United States and millions of puppies are produced by puppy mills each and every year.

But what exactly is a puppy mill, and why should you care? A puppy mill is an inhumane commercial dog breeding facility that aims to produce as many puppies as possible for the lowest cost. This means that dogs are forced to breed repeatedly until they are physically no longer capable of breeding. The dogs are kept in squalid conditions and many of them suffer from health problems and nutritional deficiencies. There is no DNA testing to prevent the spread of inherited health problems and the puppies are often separated from their mothers too early.

Again, why should you care about puppy mills? For one thing, puppy mill breeding is animal cruelty at its worst. But the way it affects you is this – when you buy a puppy mill puppy, you have no way of knowing what diseases it may have inherited from its parents and you don't know the condition it is in. All you see is a cuddly little puppy who is desperate for love. But that puppy could already be sick, which means that you may

*Photo Courtesy of Jennifer Brydges*

lose it just a few weeks or months after bringing it home. Even if your puppy lives, the chances that it will develop a serious (and expensive) health condition down the road are high.

So where should you look for French Bulldog puppies? If you are interested in rescuing a dog, check with your local animal shelter to see if they have any puppies or put in a request to be notified if they get some. You can also check online for local or regional rescues that are specific to the French Bulldog breed. Your veterinarian might have connections to a breeder and you can check the ASPCA breeder database. Various French Bulldog breed clubs may also have information about breeders.

# b.) Choosing a Responsible Breeder

Once you have collected the names and numbers of multiple French Bulldog breeders, your next step is to qualify your prospects – to narrow down your list. Start by taking your list and going online to check out the website for each breeder. Review the website thoroughly to see what kind of information is available. Responsible breeders will likely be members of the AKC or a breed-specific club and their breeding stock should be registered. You should also be able to find background information about the breeder and the facilities on the website.

After checking the website for each breeder on your list, remove any that don't appear to have a license or connection to a breed club. You should also trust your gut and remove any breeders you don't feel confident about after reviewing the information on their website. The next step is to actually contact the breeders themselves to ask a few questions. You'll want to ask about the breeder's experience with the French Bulldog breed as well as their general dog breeding experience. The breeder should be very forthcoming with information about breeding practices and any precautions taken such as DNA testing and the like.

When speaking to each breeder on your list, don't just pay attention to the answers they give to your questions – see if the breeder asks you questions as well. A responsible breeder will want to know that his or her puppies are going to a good home. You'll want to remove any breeder from your list that seems to be more concerned about making a sale than about giving the puppies a good home. You should also be wary of breeders that refuse to answer questions about their operation.

CHAPTER 3   Picking a French Bulldog Puppy

After narrowing down your list even further, pick one or two options that you like best and make an appointment to visit the facilities. It is standard practice for breeders to provide a tour of their facilities and to show prospective buyers the puppies before they make a purchase. Set an appointment to view the facilities and make sure the breeder shows you the breeding stock, the facilities in which they are kept, their health certificates, and the puppies themselves. If the facilities are unclean or if anything seems fishy to you, you should move on. It's not worth the risk to buy a puppy from an irresponsible breeder.

Photo Courtesy of Vicki Wills

## c.) Picking a Healthy French Bulldog Puppy

❝ *Ask about the parents health and if they have had a prior litter. Also, make sure a health exam is done prior to leaving the care of the breeder."*

*Jordan Mills –*
*jemfrenchbulldogs.com*

Once you've narrowed down your choices to a final breeder, all that is left is to actually pick out your puppy! Before you actually go to see the puppies available, you'll need to make a few decisions. For one thing, do you want a male or a female puppy? This is largely a matter of choice, though there are some factors to consider. For one thing, male French Bulldogs can be a little same-sex aggressive, so if you already have one at home, consider making the next one a girl. You should also take into account whether you may want to breed your dog in the future.

Next, think about what color you want your French Bulldog to be. If you've already chosen a breeder, your options might be limited as many breeders specialize in a particular color. Some French Bulldog owners maintain that dogs with a brindle pattern are the healthiest because they have a larger gene pool while pure white dogs are more likely to develop health problems. The fawn coloration is the most common and black is not an acceptable color for show. If you want a rare coloration like blue or chocolate, you may need to put your name on a waiting list.

Once you've made your decisions, you are ready to actually take a look at the puppies and pick one out. Ask the breeder to show you where the puppies are staying and then take a few moments to observe them before you start to interact. Watch the puppies to make sure that they are playful and active – lethargy is frequently a sign of disease or malaise. You'll also want to gauge the puppies' reaction to you – they should be curious and maybe a little wary, though not overly frightened.

Next, start to interact with the puppies and let them come up to sniff you. Pet the puppies gently and try to encourage them to play with a toy. You'll want to choose a puppy that you feel a connection with, so take your time to play with each puppy to see if you feel the potential for a strong bond. You'll also want to look each puppy over for signs of ill health, just to be sure that they aren't sick. Things like discharge from the

## CHAPTER 3  Picking a French Bulldog Puppy

eyes or nose, patches of irritated skin, evidence of hair loss, and aggressive behavior are all red flags when picking a puppy. Once you've made your choice, talk to the breeder about putting down a deposit if the puppy isn't quite ready to go home.

When you speak to the breeder about taking your new puppy home, be sure to ask what comes with the dog. A responsible breeder will include a contract and a health guarantee that protects you against inherited health conditions. You should also ask about what the breeder is currently feeding the puppy so you can get some of that food before transitioning your puppy to the dog food of your choice. You should also ask about any vaccinations the puppy has already received.

*Photo Courtesy of Natalie Cacciatore*

## CHAPTER 4

# Adopting a French Bulldog

The previous chapter mentioned contacting a local dog shelter to find French Bulldog puppies. In this chapter we'll delve into a little greater detail about the pros and cons of adopting a dog versus buying a puppy. Each option has its advantages and disadvantages, and what is right for one person may not be right for another. There are millions of homeless dogs looking for a home, however, so consider whether you might be willing to give a French Bulldog in need a new forever home. Keep reading to learn more about the details for adopting a dog.

## a.) Pros and Cons of Adopting a Dog

Bringing home a new puppy can be very exciting, but you need to think carefully about the challenges that come with puppyhood before you make up your mind. Adopting an adult dog is a great option for many reasons, so it is something you should seriously consider. Here is a list of pros and cons for adopting a dog that you should think about before you make your choice:

### Pros for Adopting a French Bulldog:

- Many dog shelters are forced to euthanize dogs that don't get adopted within a certain timeframe – adopting a dog could mean you are saving a life.
- Adopting a dog from a shelter is usually much less expensive than buying a puppy – the cost is usually under $250 whereas a new puppy could cost $1k+.
- Most adult dogs in the shelter system have already been housebroken and may come with some obedience training as well – that makes your job easier.
- Dog shelters generally spay and neuter their dogs before adopting them out – this could save you hundreds and can reduce your dog's risk for disease.

CHAPTER 4  Adopting a French Bulldog

- Most shelters will not adopt out a dog until it has been examined and approved by a veterinarian – the dog will also be caught up on vaccinations before adoption.
- Adult dogs in shelters have already outgrown the puppy phase which means that their personalities are more set – you will more easily be able to tell if you and the dog get along.

## Cons for Adopting a French Bulldog:

- You may not have as many options in choosing the sex or color of your French Bulldog if you choose to adopt.
- There is no guarantee that a shelter will get a French Bulldog – you may have to put your name on a list and could end up waiting quite a while.
- Many of the dogs that enter the shelter system have been abused or neglected which could lead to behavioral problems that you'll have to deal with.
- The shelter environment can be scary and stressful for dogs, so many dogs have a more subdued personality in the shelter and behavioral problems may not manifest until you get the dog home.
- Many dogs in shelters have been abandoned or found as strays so you might not know much about the dog's history, medical and otherwise.

*Photo Courtesy of Susan Sampson*

If you are willing to take the risk in adopting a French Bulldog from a shelter, good for you! It may not be the right choice for everyone, but it is a noble choice if you can make it. Keep in mind that you will be required to fill out an application to adopt a dog and may need to provide information about your housing situation and other pets you may have in the home. Shelters want to make sure that their pets get adopted out, but they also want to be sure that they are choosing the best home for each dog.

## b.) French Bulldog Puppies vs. Adults

When you are thinking about adopting a French Bulldog, you may find yourself questioning the benefits of adopting an adult dog versus buying a puppy. Aside from differences in cost, there are some other practical things to consider. Having a puppy is great, but it does mean that your life will be pretty hectic for at least the next several months. French Bulldog puppies grow very quickly but they may retain some of their puppy-like tendencies even after they reach their maximum size.

When you bring home a puppy, you should expect some challenges. The first few nights you have your puppy at home, for example, it may whine or cry because that is the first time it's been separated from its littermates. You'll also find yourself dealing with typical puppy behaviors like chewing, urinating in the house, barking or whining, and more. You can only control puppies to a certain degree, so you'll need to be prepared for that.

Though there are many obvious challenges associated with raising a puppy, there are also challenges that come with adopting an adult dog. When you adopt an adult dog, you may not know much about its previous experience with humans. Some dogs come from good homes where their previous owners became incapacitated and simply couldn't care for the dog any more. Other dogs come from homes where they were openly abused or neglected. Your dog's history will play a role in determining how it responds to you and how well it adjusts to its new life.

When you adopt a dog, you should be prepared for some rough patches. Dogs tend to be more subdued in the stressful shelter setting, so you should be ready just in case your new dog starts to show signs of behavioral problems once it settles in a little bit. You'll have to deal with these behavioral problems through consistent training and you may find that it is more difficult to re-train a dog than to start from scratch with

CHAPTER 4 Adopting a French Bulldog

a puppy, though this is not always the case. Whether you bring home a puppy or an adult, there will be an adjustment period.

## c.) Tips for Adopting a Dog

If you have made up your mind to adopt a French Bulldog, there are some preparations you should make. Before you bring the dog home, make sure you set up a space in your home that your new dog can call its own – it'll need some personal space if things become too overwhelming. You'll need to decide where your dog is allowed to go in the home and take steps to create boundaries if needed. Setting and enforcing boundaries from the get-go will be very important.

In addition to actually preparing your home for a new dog, you'll need to prep your family as well. Talk to your kids about the responsibilities involved in owning a dog and talk to them about the challenges you may face during the transition period. When you actually bring your new dog home, don't expect it to act like a member of the family right away. Give it time and space to explore its new home and to get used to new people. Some dogs will adjust more quickly than others, so just let your dog do what is right for itself. Just make sure to give your dog plenty of treats and do everything you can to foster a positive relationship from day one.

Photo Courtesy of Kathleen Smith

CHAPTER 5

# Preparing Your Home

Once you've made the decision to bring a French Bulldog puppy into your life, your next step is to prepare your home. This means puppy-proofing your house to make it a safe place for your new puppy – it also means setting up your puppy's personal space. In this chapter, you'll learn about puppy-proofing basics and you'll receive some valuable information about dangerous foods to avoid. You'll find tips for helping your Frenchie get along with other pets and you'll learn how to set up your puppy's crate so it becomes its favorite place to sleep.

Photo Courtesy of Vicki Wills

CHAPTER 5   Preparing Your Home

# a.) Puppy-Proofing Indoors and Out

Though puppy-proofing may sound silly, it is actually extremely important. French Bulldog puppies (like any puppy) are prone to getting into mischief and they don't know what things are good for them and what things are bad. It is your job to make sure that nothing in your house poses a threat to your puppy. This might mean getting rid of some things or simply putting them away in a place where your puppy can't access them. <u>Here are some things to include when puppy-proofing your home:</u>

- Make sure your trash can has a tight-fitting lid or keep it secured in a cupboard.
- Place open food containers in your pantry or cupboards or make sure they have lids.
- Put all of your cleaning products away where your puppy cannot reach them and consider locking the cabinet where you store them just to be safe.
- Remove all small objects from the floor and from places that your puppy can reach – they are a choking hazard for dogs.
- Tie or bundle electrical cords and blind cords so your puppy can't play with them.
- Keep open bodies of water covered (such as the toilet, bathtub, outdoor ponds, etc.).
- Never keep medications or other toiletries on the sink where your puppy can reach them – put them away in the medicine cabinet and use child-proof bottles.
- Check to be sure that none of the houseplants in your home or plants in your yard are toxic to dogs – if there are any, remove them, move them out of reach, or fence them off.
- Block off any fireplaces you have in the home and dispose of ashes properly.
- Keep your windows and doors securely closed when your puppy is loose; use baby gates to keep your puppy away from areas where you don't want it to be.
- Be mindful of furniture that could hurt your puppy – that includes rocking chairs, furniture with sharp edges, and the like.
- For homes with cats, keep the litter box somewhere your puppy can't reach it – puppies may be tempted to eat the clumps.

- Dispose of all food waste properly so your puppy can't get it – this is especially important for chicken bones and foods that are harmful to dogs.
- Keep all vehicle care products and lawn products safely stored away in the garage where your puppy can't reach them.
- Store lawn and garden tools where they won't fall over if your puppy bumps into them.
- Make sure that your yard is properly fenced to keep your puppy in – make sure gates are secure and that it can't fit under or between the slats.
- Avoid using chemical fertilizers, pesticides, or herbicides where your puppy could be exposed.

## b.) Dangerous Foods for Your Frenchie

It can be easy to give in to your French Bulldog puppy when it begs for scraps at the table, but you need to be aware that some people foods are dangerous for your puppy. Here is a list of foods to avoid feeding your dog:

- Alcohol
- Apple seeds
- Avocado
- Beer
- Caffeine
- Cherry pits
- Chocolate
- Coffee grounds
- Garlic
- Grapes, raisins
- Macadamia nuts
- Mold
- Mushrooms
- Mustard seeds
- Onions, leeks
- Peach, plum pits
- Potato leaves/stems
- Rhubarb leaves
- Tea
- Tomato leaves/stems
- Walnuts
- Xylitol (an artificial sweetener)
- Yeast, bread dough

CHAPTER 5 Preparing Your Home

## c.) French Bulldogs and Other Pets

*" These dogs will bark be only in very stressful situations, so the French bulldog is an excellent choice for those who are used to silence or who have sensitive neighbors!"*

*Olga Serduck*
*www.the-french-bulldogs.com*

The French Bulldog is a breed that thrives on human companionship, but that doesn't mean your dog can't get along with other pets. Most Frenchies get along with other dogs, though males of the breed can sometimes become territorial around other male French Bulldogs. If you plan to adopt a French Bulldog, it is always a good idea to schedule a preliminary playdate to see if your dogs get along. If you are planning to buy a puppy, this may not be an option, but you can always ask the breeder if you can do a trial introduction before committing to a puppy.

Photo Courtesy of Nada Smith

When it comes to other household pets, each French Bulldog is unique. These dogs are not known for having a high prey drive, though some Frenchies will chase cats. It is largely a matter of individual temperament for both your dog and your cat, so be careful when making introductions. It may help to keep your pets separated and let them get used to each other from a distance before bringing them together. You should always supervise initial interactions and separate the two if they have a problem. For the most part, however, when you raise French Bulldog puppies with other pets they get along fine.

## d.) Preparing a Space for Your Frenchie

The final thing you have to do in preparing your home for your new French Bulldog is to set up its personal space. You'll need a place to put your Frenchie's crate, so you might as well set up a separate little area that your puppy can call its own. Using a puppy playpen is a great way to do this – you can keep your puppy confined without keeping it in its crate all the time. You can also expand the play area as your puppy grows to give it a little more space. If you have a small bathroom you don't use often, you could also temporarily use that as your puppy's space until you pick a permanent spot for its crate.

When setting up your puppy's area, you should include its crate, dog bed, food and water bowls, and toys. While you are crate training your puppy, it is wise to use an old blanket or towels to make the crate a little comfier, just in case of accidents. Once your puppy is housetrained, however, you can upgrade to a more comfortable dog bed. Your puppy's food and water bowls should be nearby, but don't keep them in the crate during training – this will increase the risk for your puppy having an accident.

In preparation for crate training down the line, you should get your puppy used to the crate as soon as possible. Try tossing some treats into it and feeding your puppy meals in the crate with an open door so it forms a positive association with the crate. Eventually it'll come to recognize the crate as its own personal space and will like spending time there. Just don't use the crate as punishment.

CHAPTER 5  Preparing Your Home

Photo Courtesy of
Natalie Cacciatore

## CHAPTER 6

# The First Few Days at Home

When it's finally time to bring your French Bulldog puppy home, it can be easy to get caught up in the excitement. But you have to remember that coming to a new home can be scary and stressful for puppies, so be gentle and kind! You should also take the time to prepare your kids for the new puppy and make sure that you have all of the necessary supplies and accessories on hand. You'll learn about all of this in the following chapter and receive some tips for bringing your puppy home from the breeder, for surviving your puppy's first night at home, and for your puppy's very first visit to the vet.

## a.) Getting Kids Ready for a Puppy

The French Bulldog is a friendly and playful breed that tends to get along very well with children. Because French Bulldog puppies can be very small, however, you have to remember that they are delicate – you also have to make sure that your kids understand this fact. Taking the time to talk to your kids before you bring your new puppy home is very important. Not only do they need to learn how to safely handle the puppy, but they also need to be prepared to do the chores that are necessary to take care of a dog.

When you talk to your kids, it is important to explain to them that the puppy is not a toy – it is a living thing that deserves respect and gentle treatment. This may be more difficult for younger children to understand than older children, so adjust your strategy as needed to match the maturity level of your children. Make sure you tell your children to handle the puppy gently, to pet it softly, and to avoid making loud noises and sudden movements that could scare the puppy.

Once you've brought your new puppy home from the breeder, you may want to give the puppy some time alone to adjust. Put your puppy down in the living room and let it wander and sniff around a little bit. Once it seems to have gotten comfortable, pick it up and put it in the

CHAPTER 6 The First Few Days at Home

crate for a short nap if it seems tired. While the puppy is napping, gather your children and have them sit in a circle in the living room on the floor.

When your puppy wakes up, bring it into the room and place it on the floor in the middle of the circle. Instruct your children to wait patiently and to let the puppy come to them – make sure they don't get too loud or too excited. When the puppy approaches your children, let them pet the puppy gently on the head and back. Eventually, if your puppy seems amenable, you can help your children pick up and hold the puppy. If at any time your puppy seems to be getting frightened or overwhelmed, cut the introductions short and resume again later.

Photo Courtesy of Shianne Penoli

## b.) Initial Supplies and Accessories

> "Tour Frenchies prefer to sleep on pillows or on the couch, they don't need much space. I believe that any size home will suit them. They love to walk with the owner on a leash or harness, which is useful not only for the dog but also for the owner due to their strength!"
>
> *Elena Mikirticheva*
> *www.the-french-bulldogs.com*

If you want your Frenchie puppy to settle in to its new home quickly, you'll need to have some supplies and equipment on hand. The most important thing you need is a crate. French Bulldogs are small dogs – they generally don't weigh more than 25 to 28 pounds. This being the case, you may not need to buy a larger crate as your puppy gets bigger – you can start with one that is the right size for your adult French Bulldog. It should be just big enough for your dog to comfortably stand up, turn around, and lie down.

In addition to your puppy's crate, you'll want some old blankets or towels to make it more comfortable. Once your puppy has been housebroken you can upgrade to a nicer dog bed. You should also have a puppy playpen or some kind of barrier to block off a section of the room to keep your puppy confined when it's not in the crate. When you are away from home and when you are asleep at night, it is best to keep your puppy in the crate – at least until it is crate trained.

Other things you will need include your puppy's food and water bowls, an assortment of toys, and some grooming supplies. Food and water bowls should be proportionate to your puppy's size and should be made from stainless steel or ceramic – these are the materials that are easiest to clean and sanitize. For toys, choose a variety and let your puppy decide which ones it likes best. For grooming supplies, you'll need a brush, some dog-friendly shampoo, dog ear cleaning solution, and some nail clippers. You'll also need a collar, leash, and ID tags with your puppy's name as well as your contact information.

CHAPTER 6 The First Few Days at Home

# c.) Riding Home from the Breeder

Chances are good that your puppy's ride home from the breeder will be its very first car ride, so it might be a little scared or stressed. It can be doubly stressful if it is the first time your puppy has been separated from its littermates. Before you get into the car with your puppy, give it a chance to do its business outside – the last thing you want is to be stuck riding home with a messy car. Keep in mind that some dogs get car sick as well, so have (non-toxic) cleaning supplies on hand just in case you need them.

Some breeders recommend that you bring a box lined with blankets to transport your puppy home, or a travel crate. To make sure that your French Bulldog puppy feels safe and secure, however, you should think about wrapping it in a blanket and holding it on your lap for the duration of the trip. When your puppy gets older and becomes used to riding in the car you'll want to secure it in a travel crate or get a seatbelt-harness system to keep you both safe. For now, however, you want to make your puppy feel safe.

*Photo Courtesy of Nada Smith*

If you live more than thirty minutes away from the breeder, you may want to make a stop to let your puppy out of the car. Puppies are only capable of controlling their bladder and bowels for about one hour per month of age, but the stress of travel can lead to accidents. If you do make a stop, be sure not to expose your puppy to other dogs (or their leavings) because it may not yet be up to date on all of its shots and could be exposed to germs. Just take your puppy to a clean patch of grass and clean up after it.

# d.) The First Night at Home

In the same way that the ride home from the breeder can be stressful for your new puppy, so can the first night at home. When you first get home, give your puppy some time to explore the space you have prepared. Some puppies will be so tired out from the trip that they'll just want to take a nap – that is okay too, just keep an eye out so you can be there when it wakes up. When it does, make sure to let it outside right away.

*Photo Courtesy of Caitlyn Wilson*

CHAPTER 6  The First Few Days at Home

After your puppy has explored its area, you can allow it to expand its wandering to the rest of the home. Close doors or use baby gates to block off areas that could be hazardous for your puppy and just let it wander. Keep an eye on your puppy and watch for signs that it has to go – it will sniff the ground, circle, and start to squat. When it does, clap your hands to distract it and quickly carry it outside. If it does its business outside, praise and reward it with some tasty treats.

When bed time comes around you should play some games with your puppy to help tire it out. You'll also want to make sure it has eaten at least a few hours before so it can do its business outside before bed time. For the very first night or two, you might want to set up your puppy's crate in your bedroom so it doesn't feel so alone. It may still cry or whine a little, but avoid the temptation to let it into the bed with you unless you plan to let it sleep there for the rest of its life. Bad habits start early.

If you don't want to keep your puppy in the crate at first, give it a comfy bed to sleep in and tether it nearby so it can't wander too far. As long as you have tired it out, your puppy should sleep soundly for a few hours. If it starts to whine, it might need to go outside. Remember, puppies can only hold their bladder and bowels for a few hours at first. If your puppy is just whining for attention, you can soothe it but don't bring it into the bed or give it too much attention. If you cuddle your puppy when it whines, it'll only learn to whine more. In the morning, be sure to take your puppy out before you do anything else.

# e.) Your Frenchie's First Vet Visit

After your French Bulldog puppy has had a few days to settle in to its new home, you should take it to the vet for a checkup. This is important to do even if the breeder has given all the shots needed for its age. Your veterinarian will be able to verify that the puppy is in good health and will be able to recommend what shots are needed next and when. You'll be making several trips to the vet for shots over the next few months, so be ready for that.

When you take your new puppy to the vet it is a good idea to help it form a positive rather than a negative association – this will make every other trip easier for you. Generate some excitement with your puppy when you get in the car and give it some treats so it learns to like car rides. When you get to the vet, reward your puppy for being good – you can have the vet give it some treats too.

CHAPTER 7

# The First Month at Home

It won't take long for your French Bulldog puppy to settle in and become your new best friend. Still, caring for a puppy is no easy task and there are some important things you need to do during your puppy's first month at home to set it up well for the rest of its life. For example, even before you start training your puppy you should start enforcing certain house rules like "no jumping on the furniture" or "no begging at the table". You'll also want to start socializing your pup and think about what kind of training method you're going to use. In this chapter, you'll learn about these things and also receive an overview of the costs you can expect during your first year of dog ownership.

Photo Courtesy of Maribelle Velasco

CHAPTER 7  The First Month at Home

## a.) Enforcing House Rules

> *They do have mischievous tendencies and while these can be adorable it's important to draw the line to ensure that they know what is and is not appropriate."*
>
> *Linda*
> lovabullfrenchies.com

As is true for very young children, you can only hope to control your French Bulldog puppy to a certain degree. During that first month at home, your puppy will still be too young for serious housetraining and it won't be ready for obedience training quite yet. You can, however, start to enforce house rules right away so that your puppy doesn't develop any bad habits from a young age.

For example, unless you want your puppy to think it's okay to jump on the furniture, you shouldn't allow it at all. Each time your puppy jumps up, tell it "No" in a firm voice and place it back on the ground. If you don't want your puppy to jump into the bed, exercise the same treatment here. You should also discourage your puppy from begging for food at the table. You can do this by feeding your puppy its evening meal at the same time as your dinner or a little before; then you can put it in the crate for a nap while you eat.

In addition to enforcing house rules, you should also try to establish a routine for your puppy as soon as possible. Start the day by letting your puppy outside as soon as you get up and plan to let it out again thirty minutes after each meal and immediately after each nap. Try to stick to a regular schedule for feeding so you can predict when your puppy will need to go out – this will make things easier on you by far. And try to limit your use of treats for reinforcing desired behaviors.

## b.) Early Socialization Tips

Your French Bulldog puppy is the most impressionable during the first three to six months of its life, so this is when you want to start socializing it. The goal of socialization is to expose your puppy to a variety of situations so it learns to roll with new experiences. You want your puppy to grow up into a well-adjusted adult, so making sure it learns that new things are not to be feared is an important part of that.

Socializing your puppy is as simple as exposing it to as many new things as possible. That includes appliances around the house, new sights and sounds away from home, people of different ages and races, different modes of transportation, and even different types of animals. Your goal is to ensure that your puppy has positive experiences with all of these new things so it doesn't grow up into a fearful or nervous adult dog. If your puppy does become fearful or nervous about something during your early socialization, it is okay to comfort but not to coddle it – you don't want to give the impression that there is indeed something to be afraid of or your puppy will always respond that way to that particular situation.

## c.) Picking a Training Method

Again, your puppy is probably still too young to really start obedience training, but you can begin to lay the groundwork. Your first task is to actually decide what method of training you are going to use. Keep in mind that your ultimate goal is not just to make your dog follow your commands – it is to make your dog want to follow your commands. The French Bulldog is a very people-oriented breed that forms strong bonds with family, so as long as you and your dog have a positive bond, training shouldn't be a problem. French Bulldogs are also a very smart breed, so they tend to pick up on training very quickly – especially when treats are involved.

The best training method to use for French Bulldogs is called positive reinforcement training and it is very simple to do. All you have to do is reward your dog for desired behaviors and avoid reinforcing undesired behaviors. Basically, you give your dog a command and then lead it to perform the desired behavior – when it does, you praise and reward it to reinforce that behavior. After a few repetitions, your dog will come to associate the command with the desired behavior and repeat it on command. As long as you are consistent about using the same commands and in issuing rewards, your dog will learn new commands very quickly.

## d.) Cost Breakdown of the First Year

Owning a dog is not cheap, and many inexperienced dog owners underestimate just how much it costs to keep a dog. Not only do you have to factor in the cost of purchasing your puppy as well as all of the initial

CHAPTER 7 The First Month at Home

equipment you need, but you'll also have to pay for recurring monthly costs such as food, treats, veterinary costs, and more. To give you an idea how much you should be prepared to spend on your French Bulldog, here is a breakdown of estimated costs for the first year of dog ownership:

**Puppy Price** – The purchase price for a French Bulldog will vary greatly depending on a number of factors. The cheapest option is generally to adopt an adult dog from a shelter – that usually costs $100 to $250 and includes vaccinations and spay/neuter surgery. If you want a puppy, you should only purchase from a responsible breeder. Puppy prices for French Bulldogs tend to be fairly high, ranging from $1,400 to $2,000 – more for rare colors like blue and chocolate.

**Dog Crate** – In order to set up a special area for your puppy to call its own, you'll need a dog crate. Your puppy's crate will also play an important role in housetraining. Because the French Bulldog is a small breed, you'll probably only need a small crate – you probably won't need to upgrade to a larger one when your puppy is an adult. A small dog crate should only cost you $30 to $50.

Photo Courtesy of Jen Kemp

**Dog Bedding** – To make your puppy's crate more comfortable, you should line it with blankets or towels until it is housetrained and then upgrade to a more comfortable dog bed. You can get a small dog bed for around $20.

**Toys and Accessories** – When you first bring your puppy home, you'll want to have an assortment of different toys available so your puppy can decide what it likes. Then, just replace those favorite toys as they break or wear out. You'll also need certain accessories such as a small collar and a leash – you may also want to try a harness. You can either start with an adjustable collar or get a larger one as your puppy grows. You should plan to spend $75 to $150 on toys and accessories during the first year.

**Supplies** – In addition to toys and accessories, you'll need to have certain supplies on hand such as a bristle brush for grooming, some dog-friendly shampoo and ear cleaning solution, a pair of nail clippers, and some soft cloths for bathing. These things shouldn't cost you more than $50.

Photo Courtesy of Clarissa Clarke

CHAPTER 7 The First Month at Home

**Microchipping** – Though this is certainly not a requirement, it is definitely a good idea to have your puppy microchipped. The procedure is painless and it only costs about $30, but it can make a big difference for your Frenchie. If your dog happens to get loose, anyone who finds it can take it to a vet or shelter to scan the microchip which will be linked to your contact information.

**Veterinary Care** – When your puppy is still young, you'll need to take it to the vet every few weeks for its initial vaccinations. After the first year, it will only need booster shots once a year or every three years, depending on the vaccine. In addition to shots you should also have your puppy examined by a vet twice a year. The cost for shots will vary but you could end up spending as much as $100 the first year. You'll also be paying somewhere in the range of $25 to $45 for each vet visit.

**Spay/Neuter Surgery** – Unless you plan to breed your French Bulldog (and think very carefully before you do), you should have your pup spayed or neutered before six months of age. If you go to a regular veterinarian, spay surgery could cost up to $500, but a vet clinic will be more affordable – usually around $150 to $200. Neuter surgery is much more affordable than spay surgery, generally in the range of $50 to $100, depending on where you go.

| Estimated First Year Costs | | |
| --- | --- | --- |
| Expense | Low Cost | High Cost |
| Purchase Price | $100 | $2,000 |
| Dog Crate | $30 | $50 |
| Dog Bedding | $20 | $20 |
| Toys/Accessories | $75 | $150 |
| Supplies | $50 | $50 |
| Microchipping | $30 | $30 |
| Vaccinations | $75 | $100 |
| Spay/Neuter | $50 | $500 |
| Vet Check-Ups | $50 | $90 |
| **Year Total** | **$480** | **$2,990** |

## CHAPTER 8

# Housetraining Your French Bulldog Puppy

When your French Bulldog is still a small puppy you can't expect it to be able to hold its bladder and bowels for long. But for each month of age, it gains another hour of control. It doesn't make any sense to start housetraining your puppy until it can control itself for a few hours, but you can start as early as you like with good outdoor potty habits. In this chapter, you'll learn about the pros and cons of training your puppy to go indoors or outdoors. You'll also receive tips for supervising your puppy and a detailed step-by-step guide for crate training when your puppy is ready to make the transition.

## a.) Inside or Outside?

One of the benefits of small-breed dogs like the French Bulldog is that they are easy to keep in apartments, condos, and other small living spaces. They are also particularly popular for urban dwellers who may or may not have much outdoor green space. Many urban dwellers choose to train their dogs to go indoors on pee pads since they can't reliably take their dogs outside multiple times per day. If you choose a French Bulldog, you'll have to decide which option is right for you.

Before you decide to train your puppy to go indoors or outdoors, you need to consider a few different factors. One thing to think about is, of course, your living situation. Do you have an outdoor green space where your puppy can relieve itself? And do you have convenient access to that space as often as needed? If you live in a high-rise apartment building in an urban area, the answers to these questions may be "No". In this case, you might consider training your puppy to go indoors.

In addition to considering your living situation, you also need to think about the implications of training your Frenchie to do its business indoors. Yes, you will be training it to go on pee pads in a designated area. But you are still teaching it that it is okay to do its business indoors. Some

CHAPTER 8 Housetraining Your French Bulldog Puppy

dog lovers argue that this could increase the likelihood that your dog will have accidents indoors in unapproved locations. If you later decide to train your dog to go outdoors, you may also find it more difficult.

The benefit of training your dog to do its business outdoors is, of course, that it won't be doing it in the house. You will still be responsible for cleaning up after your dog, but you won't have to deal with the sight or smell of urine and feces inside your home. You also have the option to train your puppy to go in a designated spot in your yard to make your task of cleanup that much easier.

Photo Courtesy of Julie Preston

## b.) Keeping an Eye on Your Puppy

No matter where you choose to train your puppy to do its business, you'll have to supervise it closely throughout the training process to prevent it from having an accident in the house. Keeping your puppy on a specific feeding schedule will make it easy for you to predict when it will have to go, but you'll still need to keep an eye on it. If it starts to sniff at the floor, walk in circles, or squat, an accident is just moments away – clap your hands to distract it then pick it up and quickly take it to the designated location where it is allowed to do its business, whether indoors or out.

To make your task of supervising your puppy a little easier, try to keep it in the same room as you at all times. You can easily accomplish this by closing the door or using baby gates to keep it from leaving. Remember to take it outside (or to the designated potty spot) every hour or two so it has a chance to do its business. If it doesn't have to go, take it right back inside instead of letting it wander around, so it learns what is expected when you take it to that location.

## c.) Treats for Good Behavior

An important part of training your Frenchie to do anything is to reward it for good behavior. When it comes to housetraining, this means rewarding your puppy for doing its business in the designated area. If you are training your puppy to go in a specific area outdoors, you want to reward it for doing so – if it has a designated potty spot indoors, reward it for using that. The best thing to do is to take your puppy directly to that spot when you take it outdoors to do its business and give a verbal command like "Go pee" so it learns to associate the place with the desired action. When it uses the spot, praise it excitedly and give treats to reinforce the behavior.

Rewarding your puppy for good behavior should be applied to other aspects of training as well, not just housetraining. For example, if you want to encourage your puppy to play nicely with other household pets, praise and reward it for doing so. If you want your puppy to drop what it's chewing on when you say, "Drop it," then praise and reward it when it does that. It is really that simple – rewards are highly motivating to dogs.

# CHAPTER 8 Housetraining Your French Bulldog Puppy

Photo Courtesy of Vicki Finlay

## d.) Crate Training Tips and Tricks

> *French bulldogs are a smart breed that is quick to potty train, as long as you are consistent in your training."*
>
> *Jordan Mills*
> *jemfrenchbulldogs.com*

When you are ready to housebreak your puppy, the ideal method to use is called crate training. Basically, you teach your puppy to do its business only in one particular area and supervise it all hours of the day to ensure that it only goes in that area. When you are unable to supervise your puppy, either overnight or when you're away, you should keep it in the crate to keep it confined so it doesn't have an accident. If you teach your puppy to like the crate it will come to think of it as its den, and dogs have a natural aversion to soiling their dens.

Once you've gotten into a routine for taking your puppy outside to do its business, all you have to do is be consistent. To help you see how all of these steps work together, here is a step-by-step guide for crate training:

1. Pick a specific area of the yard where you want your puppy to do its business.
2. Take your puppy to this location every hour or two throughout the day and let it do its business, if it needs to go.
3. When you take your puppy to this spot, give it a verbal command like "Go pee" so it learns what is expected – later, once your puppy is housebroken, you can just open the door and tell it to "Go pee" and it'll go directly to the designated spot.
4. If your puppy does its business in the correct area, praise it excitedly and reward it with treats – if it doesn't have to go, just take it back inside and try again twenty minutes later.
5. Supervise your puppy closely when you are at home so it doesn't have an accident – if it shows signs that it has to go, take it outside immediately.
6. When you are unable to watch your puppy, put it in the crate or keep it confined in its area.

CHAPTER 8 Housetraining Your French Bulldog Puppy

7. Always let your puppy outside before confining it and immediately after releasing it – it will also need to go thirty minutes after a meal and immediately after waking from a nap.

In addition to following these steps, you should avoid keeping food and water with your puppy when it is confined to reduce the risk for an accident. You should also make sure not to keep your puppy confined for longer than it can hold its bladder and bowels – about one hour for each month of age.

*Photo Courtesy of Kathleen Smith*

CHAPTER 9

# Socializing Your Frenchie

As your Frenchie gets old enough for housetraining, you should also start ramping up your socialization efforts. The more experiences your puppy has while it is young, the more it will develop into a well-adjusted adult dog who greets the world with excitement rather than fear. In this chapter, you'll receive specific tips for socialization as well as information about teaching your puppy bite inhibition and proper etiquette for greeting new friends. You'll also learn about dog park etiquette which is very important if you want your puppy to interact safely and positively with other dogs.

Photo Courtesy of
Hillary Stowe

# a.) Things to Incorporate in Socialization

You've already learned about the importance of early socialization and how to get your puppy started. But it may help for you to have a list of things to include in your socialization efforts to make sure that you cover all of your bases. Here is a list of different things you should expose your French Bulldog puppy to during socialization:

## Different Types of People
- Tall people/short people
- Thin people/fat people
- People in coats
- Women in dresses
- Men with beards
- Sunglasses or hats
- Men
- Women
- Children
- Babies/toddlers
- People with glasses
- Long hair/short hair
- Different accents
- Disability/handicap
- Dancing people
- Exercising/running people

## Strange and Unfamiliar Objects
- Brooms/mops
- Flags
- Flashlights
- Strollers
- Mirrors
- Balloons
- Umbrellas
- Plastic bags
- Shopping carts
- Bicycles

## Different Types of Travel
- Car
- Bus
- Train
- Airplane
- Motorcycle
- Escalators
- Elevators
- Moving sidewalk

## Different Types of Surfaces
- Hardwood
- Tile
- Gravel
- Asphalt
- Concrete
- Bridges
- Playground

### Different Kinds of Animals

- Other dogs
- Cats
- Squirrels
- Rodents
- Birds
- Horses
- Sheep
- Chickens
- Cows
- Rabbits

### Different Places and Locations

- Airport
- Grocery store
- Dog park
- Bus station
- Shopping mall
- Outdoor park
- Dog park
- Sporting event
- Coffee shop
- School
- Parking lot
- Office
- Main road
- Dirt road

# b.) Noise Conditioning

In addition to exposing your puppy to new people and things, you should also condition it to loud noises. It is natural to be surprised by a loud noise, but you don't want your French Bulldog to grow up into the kind of dog that hides under the bed during the slightest storm. What you need to do to condition your dog to loud noises is to prevent it from forming a negative association with them – you should help it form a positive association instead by praising it for good behavior.

If you notice that your dog has already started to develop a fear of loud noises, you can try distracting it when they happen. For example, if it starts to thunder you might try engaging your dog in a game. The last thing you want to do is coddle your dog – that only teaches it that it is right to be afraid of the thing it fears. You'll just be reinforcing the fear response, making it that much more difficult to deal with in the future.

# CHAPTER 9 Socializing Your Frenchie

*Photo Courtesy of Rob Haran*

## c.) Teaching Bite Inhibition

In addition to exposing your puppy to new things, you should also teach it the rules for play. Puppies explore things with their mouths – they don't have hands like people do, so they use what they have. Unfortunately, not all puppies learn that their teeth are sharp and that biting too hard can hurt. This is called bite inhibition. Most puppies that are born to a litter and who spend at least a few weeks with their littermates naturally learn bite inhibition, but some do not.

If you have to teach your French Bulldog puppy bite inhibition, there are a few things you'll need to do. For one thing, you'll have to act like your puppy's littermates would. If you are playing with your puppy and it bites too hard, say "Ouch!" in a loud voice or you can actually make a yelping noise. Pull your hand away and stop playing with your puppy for a few seconds. After a short break, resume normal play but repeat the sequence if it happens again.

## d.) Proper Behavior at the Dog Park

> *For the most part, they do get along with other dogs as they are generally easy-going and sociable. A good key is to socialize them as puppies with other dogs, and not isolate them."*
>
> *Linda*
> *lovabullfrenchies.com*

In addition to teaching your puppy bite inhibition, you should also make sure that it displays proper etiquette at the dog park – there are also certain rules you'll need to follow. One thing you should think about teaching your dog is that it is not okay to just go running up to a strange dog – that could be dangerous for your puppy if the other dog becomes startled or is dog-aggressive. You can work with your dog to teach it to ask permission before it greets another dog. When you are out with your dog and another dog comes into view, ask your puppy to sit and hold the seated position until the other dog approaches within a few feet. Then, tell your puppy "Okay" so it can greet the dog.

At the dog park, things are entirely different – dogs will be running all over the place. This is where your puppy's socialization really comes

CHAPTER 9 Socializing Your Frenchie

into play. If it hasn't been socialized properly, it might be frightened by the other dogs. But a properly socialized Frenchie will love running and playing with the other dogs. Just make sure to follow the posted rules. Your puppy should have all of its vaccinations before it visits the dog park and it should have mastered the beginnings of obedience training – sit, stay, down, and come. If you can't control your puppy, don't take it to the dog park. And always keep an eye on your dog – don't get distracted by your phone.

Photo Courtesy of Maribelle Velasco

## CHAPTER 10

# Being the Best Puppy Parent

Raising a French Bulldog from a puppy can be challenging because you have to deal with all of that "puppy behavior" – things like chewing on your shoes, digging in the yard, and whining at all hours of the night. Another problem you may find yourself dealing with in raising a French Bulldog is separation anxiety. In this chapter, you'll learn some useful tips for dealing with problem behaviors – you'll also learn about the dangers of separation anxiety and what you can do to prevent it.

*Photo Courtesy of Tanya Norris*

CHAPTER 10 Being the Best Puppy Parent

# a.) Don't Reward Bad Behavior

Photo Courtesy of Ashley Hernandez

Being a good puppy parent is about forming a strong, positive bond with your puppy. It is also about setting boundaries and being consistent in your training. If your puppy doesn't know what you want it to do, it can't do it. French Bulldogs live to please their owners, so you need to be clear so your puppy can do what you want. One thing you should avoid doing as a puppy parent is rewarding bad behavior.

You have probably had the experience of going over to a friend's house and as soon as you walk in the door, their dog jumps all over you. Many people assume that this is a problem with the dog – that it is overly excitable or poorly trained. The real issue is with the owner. In most cases, it is an issue of reinforcing bad behavior. Think about it – when your French Bulldog puppy hops up on your lap or begs for attention, you probably coo at it and give it what it wants.

What you may not realize, however, is that you are rewarding it for doing something that you will later decide you don't want it to do. It is cute for a tiny little puppy to be jumping up at your knees, begging for attention - when your adult dog does it, it is an undesirable action. But your dog doesn't understand why the thing you once rewarded it for is now something you punish it for. This is your fault as a dog owner.

If you want your French Bulldog to be obedient and well-behaved, you have to reward it for being those things. But, more than that, you have to stop rewarding it for undesired behaviors – even if they seem silly or innocent. If you respond to your puppy's every whine or bark by paying attention to it, it's going to learn that barking and making noise gets it the attention it wants. If you find your puppy chewing on an old shoe and you turn it into a game of tug-of-war but later it gets punished for chewing on a nice shoe, your puppy is going to be confused.

## b.) Tips for Dealing with Problem Behavior

Photo Courtesy of Kim Patel

Being a responsible dog owner is about setting clear boundaries for your dog and for its behavior and then reinforcing those rules. Your puppy is going to do things you don't like, but there is a right way and a wrong way to deal with it. The worst thing you can do is to punish your puppy for doing something you don't like, especially when the punishment may not immediately follow the crime. That can be confusing for puppies. This is the problem with rubbing your puppy's nose in a pee stain hours after it had the accident – it won't understand.

The better way to deal with problem behaviors is not to punish your dog for them, but to teach your dog to exhibit positive behaviors instead. Think about this – if you find your dog chewing on your favorite shoe you will probably yell at it to stop. But then what happens? Your puppy knows that you are upset, but may not connect your anger with the action. It can be especially confusing if later you play with it with one of its chew toys. The key is to redirect undesired behaviors to a more appropriate outlet so your puppy learns exactly what is and is not allowed.

In the case of chewing, the proper course of action is to tell your puppy "No" in a firm voice and take the shoe away. But it doesn't end there.

CHAPTER 10  Being the Best Puppy Parent

You immediately give your puppy one of its favorite toys to chew on instead. When it does, you praise and reward it. If you are consistent in doing this, your puppy is going to learn that you like it when it plays with its toys, but not when it chews on your shoes. Your puppy wants to please you (and it likes treats), so it'll keep doing the thing you reward it for.

# c.) Preventing Separation Anxiety

Another issue related to behavior that is fairly common with French Bulldogs is separation anxiety. This breed is very people-oriented and Frenchies do not do well when left alone for long periods of time. Even if you do spend a good deal of time with your dog, however, some Frenchies still develop separation anxiety. Separation anxiety happens when a dog starts to display nervous and anxious behavior when it realizes you are about to leave. When you do leave, that behavior can escalate to the point where the dog becomes destructive or even attempts to escape the house. It can be very dangerous.

Because Frenchies are prone to this problem, you should take steps to prevent your puppy from becoming anxious about your leaving the house. One thing you can do is pick an extra special toy or treat that your puppy loves, but only get it out just before you leave the house. This will teach your puppy to associate your leaving the house with something positive, not something negative.

If you notice that your puppy starts to get nervous when you are preparing to leave, you might try desensitizing it to your preparations. For example, if your puppy gets nervous when you pick up your keys or put on your coat to leave, do these things and then go sit on the couch for a few minutes. Or pick up the keys, hold them for a minute, then put them back down. Over time, your puppy's anxious response will become less severe.

CHAPTER 11

# Training Your French Bulldog

As a dog owner, it is your job to make sure that you raise your French Bulldog to be obedient and well-behaved. While Frenchies generally respond well to training and they are eager to please, that doesn't mean you won't have to put in some hard work. In this chapter, you'll learn about the basics of dog training including some important dos and don'ts as well as tips for using food rewards properly. You'll also receive some insight about whether puppy obedience classes might be right for your Frenchie.

Photo Courtesy of Sean Bunevich

CHAPTER 11 Training Your French Bulldog

# a.) When Should You Start Training?

Many dog experts agree that it is never too early to start training your puppy. While you might not have much success teaching your eight-week puppy to sit, you can certainly start to set the stage for positive reinforcement training at an early age. The sooner you begin training your dog, the sooner it will start to become obedient to you and that is exactly what you want. You want your puppy to grow up into a well-behaved and obedient adult dog.

# b.) Dos and Don'ts for Dog Training

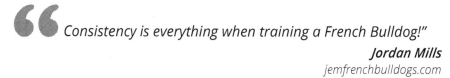

*Consistency is everything when training a French Bulldog!"*

*Jordan Mills*
*jemfrenchbulldogs.com*

Though you have the freedom to use whatever training method you choose, there are some simple rules you should follow for dog training. Rule number one is to be consistent. This applies to the commands you choose, the training sequences you follow, and the way you issue rewards. Always choose a clear verbal command that is easy to distinguish from other commands, then stick to it – if you change it, even slightly, you could confuse your puppy. You should also follow the same training sequences until your puppy identifies the desired behavior. And always praise and reward your puppy when it does what you want it to do.

The biggest "Don't" for dog training is don't punish your dog. We've already talked about how rubbing your puppy's nose in a pee stain won't teach it not to have an accident in the house. Unless the punishment immediately follows the behavior (and sometimes even then), your puppy won't make the connection and you'll just confuse it more – you might even harm your relationship, causing it to fear you or to be nervous around you. Never do anything that will put your bond with your French Bulldog in jeopardy and absolutely never abuse your dog's trust.

## c.) Using Food Rewards

Photo Courtesy of Chantel Zuza

Dogs are highly motivated by food – that is why treats are such an important part of training. But there is a right way and a wrong way to use treats. First of all, make sure that your training treats are very small – you shouldn't be giving your puppy an entire milkbone each time it performs a task correctly. Training treats should be nothing more than a bite – you don't want to overfeed your puppy or spoil its appetite for a healthy meal. In fact, you can consider using pieces of its kibble as rewards for a training session scheduled near mealtime.

Another thing to keep in mind about food rewards is that you should only use them until your puppy identifies the desired behavior. Once your puppy gets the hang of a new command, you should start phasing out the food reward so it doesn't become dependent on that. You should always praise your puppy for doing well; your praise becomes the primary reward. To keep from overusing treats, you should start using them only every other time your puppy performs correctly, then every third time, then just stick to praise.

## d.) Puppy Preschool – Yay or Nay?

As you start training your French Bulldog puppy you will come to see that it is quite the undertaking. These dogs are very smart and eager to please, but they also have a lot of energy and puppies are always a challenge to control. This being the case, you may start to wonder whether you should enroll your puppy in obedience classes or if you should hire a private trainer. The idea of hiring a trainer might sound good because it will save you from doing the hard work, but the truth is that your puppy will learn to respond to the trainer's commands – you'll still have to work with it so that it will respond to you.

CHAPTER 11 Training Your French Bulldog

Puppy obedience classes are great for a number of reasons. For one thing, they help newbie dog owners learn the proper way to train their puppies. These classes are also a great chance to socialize your puppy to new people and to other dogs. Just remember that you still have to work with your puppy outside of class to solidify its response – you can't just do one hour of training per week. It should be something you do every day, two or three times a day. But keep your training sessions short and fun – about fifteen minutes each is good.

Photo Courtesy of Laura Taylor

## CHAPTER 12

# Teaching the Basics

Now that you understand the basics of dog training you're ready to get down to the details of how to do it. To start this chapter off, you'll first learn about the importance of obedience training. Then we'll get into the specifics for how to teach your French Bulldog the basic commands of sit, down, come, and stay. After that, we'll talk about some options to reinforce your dog's training and to take things up a notch. With the right training methods, you can teach your dog to do just about anything!

*Photo Courtesy of Sophie Hughes*

CHAPTER 12 Teaching the Basics

# a.) Why is Obedience Important?

*Photo Courtesy of Julie Preston*

The thought of having an obedient and well-behaved dog is one that every dog owner likes. But it takes a lot of work to get there. As you struggle to train your French Bulldog, it may help for you to think about exactly why obedience is so important. It shouldn't be about bringing your dog to heel or establishing yourself as the alpha dog of the household – it is about doing what is best for your dog.

Imagine this – you live in a nice neighborhood near a busy street. One day you come home from the grocery store and you open the front door. Your dog sees you coming and immediately bursts through, brushing past you and rushing out across the lawn. As it approaches the street, seemingly oblivious to anything other than its unexpected adventure, a car barrels down the road. In that moment, your dog is unaware of the fact that its life could be ended with a sudden impact.

In situations like this, having the ability to call your dog back could very well save its life. A properly trained dog will respond to its owner's commands consistently and completely. It certainly takes time to reach that point, and you will have to reinforce your dog's training throughout its life, but it is definitely worth the effort. Your dog's life is worth the effort.

# b.) Sit, Down, Come and Stay

Now that you understand the importance of obedience, you are ready to learn how to train your French Bulldog to follow the four basic commands: Sit, Down, Come, and Stay. Below you will find simple training sequences to follow for each of these commands.

### Command: Sit

Begin by kneeling in front of your French Bulldog and hold a small treat between the thumb and forefinger of your dominant hand. Hold the treat just in front of your Frenchie's nose so it can smell it then say "Sit" in a firm tone of voice. Immediately move your hand forward and up toward the back of your puppy's head. Its nose will lift to follow the treat and its bottom will lower to the floor. When its bottom hits the floor, tell your puppy "Good dog!" and give it the treat. Repeat this sequence a few times until your puppy gets the hang of it.

### Command: Down

Begin by kneeling in front of your French Bulldog and hold a small treat between the thumb and forefinger in your dominant hand. Hold the treat just in front of your Frenchie's nose so it can smell it then tell it to "Sit" in a firm tone of voice. After your puppy sits, then give the "Down" command. Immediately move your hand down to the floor between your puppy's feet. Its nose will follow the treat and the rest of its body should follow. When its belly hits the floor, tell your puppy "Good dog!" and give it the treat. Repeat this sequence a few times until your puppy gets the hang of it.

### Command: Stay

Begin by kneeling in front of your French Bulldog and hold a small treat between the thumb and forefinger in your dominant hand. Hold the treat just in front of your Frenchie's nose so it can smell it then say "Sit" in a firm tone of voice. When your puppy sits, then give the command "Stay" and take a quick step backward. If your puppy stays, tell it "Good dog" and move forward to give it the treat. Repeat the sequence, moving back a few more steps each time. As long as your puppy responds consistently, keep rewarding it.

### Command: Come

Begin by kneeling in front of your French Bulldog and hold a small treat between the thumb and forefinger of your dominant hand. Hold the treat just in front of your Frenchie's nose so it can smell it then say "Sit" in a firm tone of voice. When your puppy sits, then tell it to "Stay". Take a few steps backward then clap your hands excitedly and tell your puppy to "Come". If it does, tell it "Good dog" and give it the treat. Keep practicing this command at different distances and in different settings to test your dog's obedience.

CHAPTER 12 Teaching the Basics

# c.) Taking Your Training Up A Notch

Once your French Bulldog puppy has mastered the four basic commands, you can teach it to do just about anything. The thing to remember is that your puppy can only do what you want if it knows what that is. Review the four basic commands again and see how each training sequence involves a series of actions that shows your dog exactly what you want it to do. When you are ready to teach your puppy a new trick, develop a sequence of motions that will teach your puppy to do the desired thing and then reinforce it with praise and rewards.

Photo Courtesy of Shianne Penoli

## CHAPTER 13

# Feeding Your French Bulldog

While some might argue that training your dog is your biggest responsibility as a dog owner, feeding your dog a healthy diet may be even more important. Without a healthy diet, your dog won't be healthy – it's as simple as that. In this chapter, you'll learn about the importance of a healthy diet and you'll learn all you need to know about canine nutritional needs. Then we'll discuss the proper way to shop for dog food and explore some of the dangers associated with obesity in dogs.

## a.) Why is a Healthy Diet Important?

Your French Bulldog's body is like a machine. It is made up of different parts and systems that all work together. Each part and system requires fuel in order to do its job, and that fuel is a healthy diet. Without a healthy diet, your dog's body won't have the nutrients it needs to support basic functions and your dog won't be healthy. The effects of an improper diet can compound over time, leading to serious nutritional deficiencies and other health problems.

Fortunately, choosing a healthy diet for your French Bulldog is easy. All you have to do is learn the basics about canine nutrition and then apply that knowledge to your selection of a commercial dog food product. Commercial dog foods, much like food for people, all come in packages that contain the information you need to make a smart choice. You'll learn more about reading a dog food label later in this chapter.

CHAPTER 13  Feeding Your French Bulldog

*Photo Courtesy of Ashley Hernandez*

## b.) Canine Nutritional Needs

> *The teeth of the French bulldogs are quickly worn and are not strong, so it is better to give them bones very rarely."*
>
> *Elena Mikirticheva*
> *www.the-french-bulldogs.com*

All living things need a balance of nutrients in order to survive. For dogs, like for humans, the three most important nutrients are protein, fat, and carbohydrate. It is important to note that the ideal ratio for these nutrients is very different for dogs than for humans. The average human diet is very carbohydrate-heavy because the human body is designed to utilize glucose as its primary source of fuel. Dogs, on the other hand, are designed for a more meat-based diet. They are not obligate carnivores like cats are, but the majority of their nutrition should come from animal-based sources, both proteins and fats.

If you want to know exactly what to look for in a healthy diet for dogs, you should consider the minimum requirements for protein and fat. Growing puppies, as well as pregnant and lactating females, have higher requirements for protein and fat than adult dogs. A balanced diet for puppies should consist of at least 22% protein and 8% fat. For adult dogs, those minimums are 18% and 5%. Keep in mind, however, that more is always better when it comes to these requirements.

Protein is made up of amino acids and it plays a role in developing healthy tissues and muscles. There are twenty-two different amino acids that a dog needs in its diet, but it is capable of synthesizing (producing) only twelve of them. The remaining ten are known as essential amino acids because they must come from the diet. Animal-based proteins like meat, poultry, eggs, and fish are considered complete proteins because they contain all ten of these essential amino acids.

Fats play an important role in a dog's diet because they are the most highly concentrated source of energy available. Proteins and carbohydrates each contain four calories per gram – a calorie is simply a unit of energy. Fat, on the other hand, contains nine calories per gram. This is especially important to know for small-breed dogs like the French Bulldog because they actually have higher energy needs than larger dogs. Small

## CHAPTER 13 Feeding Your French Bulldog

dogs have very fast metabolisms so they burn more calories per pound of bodyweight than larger dogs. For this reason, commercial dog foods that are formulated for small dogs tend to be higher in fat.

When it comes to carbohydrate, dogs have no specific requirements. Certain carbohydrates can provide energy, but they are more valuable as a source of dietary fiber to support your dog's healthy digestion. It is important to remember, however, that your dog's body can more efficiently process and digest animal-based foods than plant-based foods, so you should limit your dog's carbohydrate intake. A high-quality commercial dog food won't contain any more than 5 percent crude fiber.

Your dog also needs an assortment of vitamins and minerals in its diet. Fortunately, commercial dog foods are required to meet certain nutritional minimums in order to be sold as a staple diet. The American Association of Feed Control Officials (AAFCO) is the governing body that controls this. If a dog food product contains an AAFCO statement of nutritional adequacy, you can rest assured that it will provide for your Frenchie's basic nutritional needs in terms of the three core nutrients and vitamins and minerals.

# c.) Choosing a Healthy Dog Food

*French Bulldogs often have more food sensitivities then some other breeds, so it is important to feed a high-quality food that is easier to digest and has as few fillers (corn and by-products) as possible."*

*Linda*

*lovabullfrenchies.com*

Now that you understand the basics about canine nutrition, you should have a better idea of what to look for when it comes time to shop for your French Bulldog's food. If you look nowhere else on the dog food label, be sure to check the ingredients list. The ingredients lists for dog foods are written in descending order by volume – this means that the ingredients at the top of the list are used in higher quantities than those at the bottom of the list. So you want to see high-quality ingredients at the top.

If you remember the fact that most of your dog's nutrition should come from animal-based sources, it should make sense that you want to see high-quality sources of animal protein at the top of the ingredient list for any dog food you choose. Some quality sources include things like chicken, turkey, salmon, and other meats, poultry, and fish. Don't be thrown off by the word "meal" here – meat meals are simply fresh meats that have been cooked to remove moisture which makes them a more highly concentrated source of protein.

After high-quality meats, you want to see some animal-based fats on the list. Things like chicken fat and salmon oil are great choices. Plant-based fats like flaxseed are okay because they help to ensure a balance of omega-3 and omega-6 fatty acids, but just remember that animal-based ingredients are preferable. Avoid hydrogenated plant oils and unnamed fats like "animal fat". If the ingredient comes from an unnamed source, you have no way of judging its quality so it probably isn't something you want to feed your French Bulldog.

When it comes to carbohydrates, you want to see that they are digestible sources. Whole grains like brown rice and oatmeal are generally considered digestible for dogs, but keep in mind that French Bulldogs are prone to food allergies – particularly grain allergies. You may want to look for gluten-free and grain-free options like sweet potato, tapioca, or beans and legumes. And remember, the dog food should be high in protein and fat with limited carbohydrate content and no more than 5% crude fiber.

One of the easiest ways to choose a quality dog food is to buy one that is formulated for a dog of the right size. As mentioned earlier, small-breed dog foods are higher in fat than other foods to meet the high-energy needs of smaller dogs. If you choose a reputable brand of dog food you can trust that one of their small-breed formulas will be a good choice for your Frenchie. Choose a high-quality small-breed puppy food for your puppy until it reaches about 80 percent of its adult size. Then you should switch to a small-breed adult food – ideally one from the same brand, or even the same formula, to reduce any digestive problems that might result from a change in diet.

CHAPTER 13 Feeding Your French Bulldog

# d.) The Dangers of Obesity

In addition to choosing a high-quality dog food product for your French Bulldog, you should also be mindful of how much you are feeding it. Obesity is very dangerous for dogs, especially for smaller breeds where a gain of one or two pounds can be significant. Your best bet is to follow the feeding instructions on the pet food label according to your dog's weight.

Follow those instructions for a few weeks while carefully monitoring your dog's weight and condition. If it loses weight or becomes lethargic, you might want to increase its daily ration a little bit. If it gains too much weight, scale back. Your veterinarian will be able to help you determine what is a healthy weight for your dog.

Photo Courtesy of
Karen Moe

CHAPTER 14

# Grooming Your French Bulldog

> *Frenchies don't shed much, but twice a year (spring and fall) they will lose their undercoat"*
>
> **Linda**
> *lovabullfrenchies.com*

The French Bulldog is typically considered a low-maintenance breed for a number of reasons. In addition to having fairly low needs for exercise compared to some breeds, Frenchies also have short coats that are easy to maintain. In this chapter, you'll learn the basics about grooming your French Bulldog including information about recommended grooming tools, tips for brushing and bathing your dog, and instructions for keeping its ears clean and nails trimmed.

## a.) Recommended Grooming Tools

The French Bulldog has a short, fine coat that is very easy to groom. These dogs shed moderately, but you may not notice since the hairs are so short. This breed does shed its undercoat twice a year, so you'll notice more shedding during the spring and fall. You may need to do some extra brushing at this time, ideally with a stripping comb, to remove the excess hair. The rest of the year, however, you can get by with a soft bristle brush.

In addition to brushing your French Bulldog, you'll also need to bathe it occasionally when it gets dirty. It's also your job to brush its teeth, to trim its nails, and to clean its ears. For all of these grooming tasks you'll need certain supplies including dog-friendly shampoo, a dog toothbrush, dog-friendly toothpaste, nail clippers, and dog ear cleaning solution. You can find all of these products at your local pet store.

CHAPTER 14 Grooming Your French Bulldog

# b.) Brushing and Bathing

You'll want to brush your Frenchie several times a week to control shedding and to help distribute the natural oils produced by its skin to keep its coat soft. Use a soft bristle brush and start at the base of your dog's neck, working your way down the back and along the sides, always moving in the direction of hair growth. Brush down each of your dog's legs and don't forget the fur on the chest and abdomen. Because the Frenchie's coat is so short, you shouldn't have to worry about tangles.

French Bulldogs don't tend to spend a lot of time rolling around in the mud, but they can get into mischief and mischief sometimes gets dirty. When your Frenchie needs a bath, just plop it into a bathtub filled with a few inches of lukewarm water. Squeeze a little dog-friendly shampoo into your hand then work it into your dog's coat until it lathers nicely, keeping its face and ears dry. Rinse your dog thoroughly until all traces of soap are gone, then towel dry.

Photo Courtesy of Kim Patel

In addition to bathing your Frenchie as needed, you'll also need to keep its skin folds clean and dry. Use a damp cloth or a mild baby wipe to clean out the folds on its face and body then use a towel to make sure the skin is completely dry – moist skin folds become a breeding ground for bacteria. Needs will vary from one dog to another, but you should plan to clean your Frenchie's skin folds a few times per week. Don't forget to clean the pocket under its tail as well, though some Frenchies don't have one.

## c.) Trimming the Nails

Trimming your Frenchie's nails is a simple enough task, but there is a right way and a wrong way to do it. What you need to remember is that each of your dog's nails contains a quick – that is the blood vessel that supplies blood to the nail. You can see the quick if you look closely at your dog's nails, depending what color they are. When you clip your Frenchie's nails, just clip the tip – avoid cutting too close to the quick because it will hurt your dog and it will bleed profusely. Keep some styptic powder on hand to stop the bleeding if you make a mistake and cut too close.

## d.) Cleaning Your Dog's Ears

The French Bulldog is easy to identify by its large, bat-like ears. In addition to being an iconic part of the breed's appearance, the French Bulldog's ears have a lower risk for ear infections than other breeds because they are erect and open to the air. When a dog's ears hang down on either side of its head, moisture can be trapped inside which can allow infection-causing bacteria to multiply. Still, you should clean your Frenchie's ears about once a week, or as needed. Simply squeeze a few drops of dog ear cleaning solution into the ear canal then massage the base of the ear to distribute the solution. Then wipe away the solution, along with any ear wax or debris, using a clean cotton pad.

## e.) Brushing Your Frenchie's Teeth

The final aspect of keeping your Frenchie groomed involves brushing its teeth. It may sound like a silly idea to brush your dog's teeth, but dogs are just as prone to periodontal disease as humans. In fact, about

CHAPTER 14 Grooming Your French Bulldog

30% of dogs exhibit some degree of dental disease by the time they are one year old. You'll want to brush your dog's teeth as often as it will let you. Starting while it is still a puppy is the best way to get it used to this kind of treatment.

You should start by getting your French Bulldog puppy used to having its teeth and gums touched – you can do this several times a day with your finger, giving your dog a small treat and plenty of praise to encourage it to allow this. After a week or so, start touching your dog's teeth with a dog toothbrush so it gets used to that sensation. Eventually you can add a little bit of toothpaste and brush a few of your dog's teeth at a time, working your way up to brushing its entire mouth after each meal.

Photo Courtesy of Tina Reynolds

## CHAPTER 15

# French Bulldog Healthcare

One of your most important roles as a French Bulldog owner is to make sure that your dog gets the care it needs – this includes veterinary care. If you buy your puppy from a breeder, it will probably already have some vaccinations under its belt by the time you bring it home – the same is true if you adopt an adult dog. But you still need to take your dog to the vet several times a year for checkups and for booster shots. You'll learn all about your Frenchie's healthcare requirements in this chapter including tips for routine veterinary care, advice for parasite prevention, important information about heartworms, and details about common conditions affecting the French Bulldog breed.

*Photo Courtesy of Sean Bunevich*

CHAPTER 15  French Bulldog Healthcare

Photo Courtesy of Laura Taylor

## a.) Routine Veterinary Care

As much as you may want to, you can't completely protect your French Bulldog from disease. There are vaccinations for some of the most common canine diseases, but others cannot be prevented if your dog is exposed. What you can do to help keep your dog healthy is take it to the vet for regular checkups – twice a year is recommended. You should also keep an eye on your Frenchie's behavior because changes in behavior are often an indicator of a health problem in dogs.

When you take your Frenchie to the vet, he or she will perform a thorough physical exam. At this time, tell your vet about any concerns you have, even if they seem minor. Your vet will be checking your dog's weight, body condition, and various other aspects of its health to see if anything has changed since the last visit. It is very important to keep up-to-date with these exams because the earlier you catch a disease, the sooner you can start treatment and the more likely your dog is to make a full recovery.

## b.) Preventing Fleas and Ticks

Another important aspect of caring for your Frenchie's health is to protect it against parasites such as fleas and ticks. Do not make the mistake of thinking that ticks are only a problem during the summer months – they are certainly more common in warm weather but can latch on to your dog at any time of year. A good topical flea and tick preventative will help to keep new parasites from latching on, keep eggs from hatching, and keep adults from biting your dog. Because fleas and ticks can transmit dangerous diseases, this is very important. Some of the diseases that ticks can carry include Lyme disease and Rocky Mountain Spotted Fever.

*Photo Courtesy of Jen Kemp*

CHAPTER 15 French Bulldog Healthcare

## c.) What is Heartworm?

In addition to worrying about fleas and ticks biting your dog, you should also be aware that mosquitoes pose a threat. The actual bite of a mosquito is unlikely to bother your dog much, but mosquitoes can carry deadly heartworms. Heartworms can develop and grow inside your dog's heart and be spread throughout the body, causing progressive organ damage, lung disease, and even heart failure. Heartworms are particularly dangerous because they take several months to grow so you won't see any signs of a problem until it is too late.

Heartworm can only be transmitted through mosquito bites. Mosquitoes ingest baby heartworms when they feed on an infected animal. The larvae then develop inside the mosquito over the next 10 to 14 days and when the mosquito bites a dog, the larvae are transmitted into the dog's bloodstream. Over the next six months, the larvae develop into adult heartworms, causing symptoms such as exercise intolerance, persistent cough, decreased appetite, and unexplained weight loss.

Heartworms can live inside your dog for as long as five to seven years, so you need to start your French Bulldog puppy on a heartworm preventative as early as possible. You can start a puppy under the age of seven months with heartworm preventatives at any time. However, if the puppy is older than seven months you'll need to have it tested before starting the preventative. If your puppy starts before seven months of age you should still have it tested after six months because it takes that long for the heartworms to multiply and develop to a detectible level.

## d.) Vaccinating Your Frenchie

In order to protect your French Bulldog from common diseases, you'll need to have it vaccinated. While your puppy is young, it will need several sets of shots to establish immunity. After that, an annual booster shot will suffice for most things. Your veterinarian will be able to tell you exactly which shots are needed and when, but here is a general vaccination schedule for dogs:

| Dog Vaccination Schedule | | | |
|---|---|---|---|
| **Vaccine** | **Doses** | **Age** | **Booster** |
| Rabies | 1 | 12 weeks | Annual |
| Distemper | 3 | 6 to 16 weeks | 3 Years |
| Parvovirus | 3 | 6 to 16 weeks | 3 Years |
| Adenovirus | 3 | 6 to 16 weeks | 3 Years |
| Parainfluenza | 3 | 6 weeks, and 12 to 14 weeks | 3 Years |
| Bordetella | 1 | 6 weeks | Annual |
| Lyme Disease | 2 | 9 weeks, and 13 to 14 weeks | Annual |
| Leptospirosis | 2 | 12 and 16 weeks | Annual |
| Canine Influenza | 2 | 6 to 8 weeks, and 8 to 12 weeks | Annual |

# e.) Common Frenchie Health Problems

> *French Bulldogs commonly suffer from dysplasia of the hip joint and the formation of "wedge-shaped vertebrae", which manifest themselves in adulthood. To identify these diseases, breeders are advised to take DNA testing for the parents of future puppies."*
>
> *Olga Serduck*
> *www.the-french-bulldogs.com*

Unfortunately, the French Bulldog is prone to a number of health problems. Some of these health problems are congenital conditions that can be passed from mother to puppy and others are related to the breed's shortened facial structure. As you learned in the first chapter of this book, the conditions to which the French Bulldog breed is most prone include hip dysplasia, allergies, patellar luxation, intervertebral disc disease, von Willebrand's disease, elongated soft palate, and brachycephalic syndrome.

## CHAPTER 15  French Bulldog Healthcare

Hip dysplasia and patellar luxation are both musculoskeletal problems. Hip dysplasia occurs when the head of the femur (thigh bone) slips out of its original position in the hip socket. Similarly, patellar luxation occurs when the knee cap (patella) slips out of position, or luxates. Both of these conditions can cause symptoms such as altered gait, limping, reluctance to exercise or climb stairs, joint inflammation, and pain. Left untreated, these conditions can sometimes cause progressive damage to the joint which can contribute to arthritis or even cause lameness in the affected limb.

Brachycephalic syndrome is actually a group of anatomical abnormalities known to affect dog breeds with shortened facial structures. These abnormalities may include an elongated soft palate, a hypoplastic trachea, stenotic nares, and everted laryngeal saccules. Stenotic nares are abnormally small nostrils which can restrict airflow and elongated soft palate can block the entrance to the trachea, impairing airflow into the windpipe. A hypoplastic trachea is a smaller trachea than normal and everted laryngeal saccules are small sacs located inside the larynx which can be sucked into the airway, causing breathing problems.

Von Willebrand's disease is one of the most common inherited blood clotting disorders in dogs. It occurs due to a deficiency in von Willebrand factor (vWF) which leads to excessive bleeding, even with minor injuries. Intervertebral disc disease mimics the symptoms of a ruptured disc and can lead to pain in the neck and back, altered gait, weakness, and even lameness or paralysis. French Bulldogs are also prone to allergies, particularly food allergies, so you may need to feed your dog a special diet.

# CHAPTER 16
# Travel Tips for Frenchies

Because the French Bulldog is a small dog, it is easy to bring your pup with you on car trips. As long as you get your puppy used to riding in the car fairly early, it should learn to like it and you won't have problems in the future. In order to keep your pup safe in the car, you'll need to buy a travel carrier or invest in a seatbelt-harness system. In this chapter, you'll learn about some travel safety tips for your French Bulldog. You'll also learn about the pros and cons of kennels vs. pet sitters for the times when you can't bring your Frenchie with you.

Photo Courtesy of Natalie Cacciatore

CHAPTER 16 Travel Tips for Frenchies

# a.) Basic Car Safety Tips

While your French Bulldog might be perfectly happy to sit on the front seat next to you, it is generally not safe to let your dog wander around the car while you're driving. One option is to buy a travel carrier for your dog. They make travel seats for small dogs that work almost like a booster seat – it is a box that sits on the seat and straps in with the seatbelt. You then place your dog in the box and use a clip to secure it in the seat. You can also use a traditional travel carrier and keep it in the back seat. Another option is to buy your Frenchie a harness that comes with a strap or buckle to attach to the seatbelt.

When you take your Frenchie with you in the car, make sure that the temperature is appropriate. Remember that its shortened face can sometimes lead to breathing problems, especially in hot weather. In hot weather, keep the air conditioning turned on and try to point a vent at your dog to keep it cool. Never leave your dog in the car alone, even if it is for just a few minutes and you leave the window cracked. It only takes a few minutes for the temperature in your car to become dangerous and your Frenchie could suffocate if you're not careful. Unless you can bring your Frenchie wherever you are going, do not bring it along.

*Photo Courtesy of Maribelle Velasco*

## b.) Traveling with Your Frenchie

If you are travelling with your Frenchie by car, be sure to bring everything your dog will need. This includes food, water, pooper scooper bags, and whatever you need to keep your pup safe in the car. Be sure to take a break every few hours so your Frenchie can do its business and stretch its legs. If you have to go inside during a rest break, have someone stay in the car with your dog and take turns going in – don't leave it alone.

*Photo Courtesy of Shianne Penoli*

If you plan to travel with your Frenchie on a trip that is too far to drive, you can consider taking it with you on the plane. Some airlines will allow small dogs to be kept in a crate in the cabin while others require dog crates to be checked along with the luggage. Check with the airline ahead of time to determine their policy and to make arrangements for your dog – most airlines only allow a certain number of pets on each flight. You'll also need to make sure that the carrier you buy is approved by that specific airline.

## c.) Home Away from Home

Taking your pup with you on vacation can be great, but it does come with some challenges. Some dogs do not adjust well to staying in hotels and other places that are unfamiliar. You can help to make the hotel feel more like home for your dog by bringing its dog bed or preferred bed-

CHAPTER 16 Travel Tips for Frenchies

ding as well as some favorite toys. You should also make sure to bring its dog bowls as well as whatever food is needed and some treats.

To make your dog's hotel stay a little more comfortable, ask for a ground floor room so you don't have to navigate stairs or use the elevator. As soon as you get to the hotel, check out the grounds to determine the best place to take your dog to do its business – and always clean up after it! Make sure to call ahead as well to double-check the hotel's pet policy, just to be safe. And don't forget to ask about any pet fees they may charge.

## d.) Kennels vs. Pet Sitters

Photo Courtesy of Sarah Simpson

If you must travel and can't take your French Bulldog with you, you'll need to decide whether to board it at a kennel or to hire a pet sitter to care for it at home. While some kennels are designed to look like doggie hotels, others consist of little more than chain-link cages with hard cement floors. Be sure to check out any kennel before you board your dog, and ask about the services they provide. Some kennels only provide one walk per day while others have fenced outdoor space where the dogs can stretch their legs and get out of their kennels.

Because French Bulldogs are a people-oriented breed, they may not do well in a kennel environment. If you want to make sure that your dog gets the best care while you are away, consider hiring an in-home dog sitter. Pet sitters offer a variety of services including walks and multiple daily check-ins. Some will even stay in the home with your dog overnight. Be prepared to pay for these services but know that your dog may be more comfortable in its own home (even if you are not there) than at a kennel.

# Conclusion

    Nothing is more adorable than a French Bulldog contentedly curled up by your side. These little dogs are full of love and bursting with personality – they are just as goofy as they are loving. But owning a French Bulldog, like owning any dog, does come with challenges. What you need to decide is whether you are up to the challenge and whether you can give a French Bulldog the kind of life and love that it deserves. If you can, you will find that your Frenchie becomes your most loyal friend and companion. So, if you're ready to take that step, take what you've learned here and put it to work to become the best French Bulldog owner you can possibly be!

Made in the USA
San Bernardino, CA
28 December 2019